HOW
VIRTUAL
REALITY
WILL IMPACT SOCIETY

by Cecilia Pinto McCarthy

ReferencePoint
Press®

San Diego, CA

TECHNOLOGY'S
IMPACT

© 2019 ReferencePoint Press, Inc.
Printed in the United States

For more information, contact:
ReferencePoint Press, Inc.
PO Box 27779
San Diego, CA 92198
www.ReferencePointPress.com

LIBRARY OF CONGRESS CATALOGING-IN-PUBLICATION DATA

Name: McCarthy, Cecilia Pinto, author.
Title: How Virtual Reality Will Impact Society / by Cecilia Pinto McCarthy.
Description: San Diego, CA : ReferencePoint Press, Inc., [2019] | Series:
   Technology's Impact | Audience: Grades 9 to 12. | Includes bibliographical references and index.
Identifiers: LCCN 2018013680 (print) | LCCN 2018014600 (ebook) | ISBN
   9781682825020 (ebook) | ISBN 9781682825013 (hardback)
Subjects: LCSH: Virtual reality—Social aspects—Juvenile literature.
Classification: LCC HM851 (ebook) | LCC HM851 .M39295 2019 (print) | DDC
   006.8—dc23
LC record available at https://lccn.loc.gov/2018013680

Contents

IMPORTANT EVENTS IN THE DEVELOPMENT OF
VIRTUAL REALITY

1961
Two engineers at the Philco Corporation in Philadelphia, Pennsylvania, invent Headsight, a motion-tracking headset for military pilots.

1984
Jaron Lanier founds VPL Research, a company that develops virtual reality hardware and software.

1957
Cinematographer Morton Heilig invents a multisensory simulator called the Sensorama.

1995
Nintendo releases the Virtual Boy game console, the first VR machine for at-home gaming.

1835	1955	1970	1985	2000

1838
British scientist Charles Wheatstone invents the stereoscope, a device that uses two mirrors to create a 3D image.

1968
Ivan Sutherland invents the Sword of Damocles, the first virtual reality headset connected to a computer.

1987
Jaron Lanier of VPL Research popularizes the term *virtual reality*.

2012
Inventor Palmer Luckey begins a Kickstarter fundraising campaign to fund the production of his Oculus Rift virtual reality headset.

2015
Samsung starts publicly selling a testing version of the Gear VR headset which works with the Samsung Galaxy Note 4 smartphone.

2007
The University of Reading in England recreates a virtual warzone in an effort to help veterans suffering from post-traumatic stress disorder (PTSD).

2014
Google releases Google Cardboard, an inexpensive VR device that uses smartphones and smartphone apps to produce virtual reality experiences.

2016
The world's first virtual reality surgery is live streamed from the Royal London hospital in England.

2007	2010	2013	2016	2019

2008
Professor Stephen O'Leary develops a VR surgery simulator to help medical students practice surgical techniques.

2014
Mark Zuckerberg, founder of Facebook, buys Oculus Rift for $2 billion.

2018
Florida's Ringling College of Art and Design becomes the first art college to offer a degree in virtual reality development.

2016
Several technology companies release consumer VR headsets, including Oculus Rift, Sony PlayStation VR, and HTC Vive.

2018
The US alpine ski team becomes the first known Olympic team in the world to use virtual reality for training.

Virtual Reality Today

In February 2018, students at Danville High School in Illinois drove around a tree-lined street and through heavy city traffic without leaving school. Instead of real cars, the students used virtual reality (VR) **simulators**. AT&T, a telecommunications company, brought the VR simulators to Danville as part of launching its 2018 nationwide "It Can Wait" campaign, geared at reducing distracted driving. According to the US Centers for Disease Control and Prevention (CDC), car accidents are the leading cause of death for American teenagers. Distracted driving is a major cause of accidents involving teen drivers. AT&T's "It Can Wait" **initiative** uses virtual reality experiences to show students just how dangerous texting and driving can be.

The Danville students took turns using the simulators to experience the consequences of distracted driving. Students wore special goggles and headphones to create the virtual experience. As a driver drove through a virtual neighborhood, he faced a variety of distractions. When a phone began to buzz with messages, the driver took his eyes off the road. The simulation ended in a shower of broken glass from a collision. The "It Can Wait" campaign brought VR simulators to events, colleges, and other high schools after launching at Danville. The program's creators hope that these realistic demonstrations can prevent real-world tragedies.

The driving simulator works by having a computer program transmit video to a person's VR headset. The display inside the headset shows two side-by-side images of the same scene from slightly different angles. Lenses in front of each eye bend the light from the display in a way that tricks the eyes into thinking the screen is farther away. A tracking system in the headset senses the user's movements. The virtual reality system changes the image and sound in response to the user's actions. Sounds coming from the headset enhance the user's feeling of being present in the virtual world.

Traditional driving education programs use a combination of classroom learning and on-the-road experiences to prepare new drivers. But training with virtual reality has proven to be more effective. Educators believe that experiencing a virtual crash caused by distracted driving has a greater impact on students than just talking about the dangers. Even though drivers behind the wheel of the simulator aren't really traveling anywhere, everything about the experience feels real. "This is a safe way for young people to understand the consequences of distracted driving," says Chris Warwick of AT&T.[1]

Jim Graham manages a driver education program produced by Ford Motor Company called Ford Driving Skills for Life. He believes using VR will likely feel natural to teens who grew up using computers, smartphones, and other electronics as learning devices. "Virtual reality is the ideal medium to highlight the dangers of distracted driving to young motorists. This age group is more likely to engage with VR," Graham says.[2]

The market for using VR for driver education goes beyond distracted driver experiences. With VR, teen and adult students can

Experts believe virtual reality driving simulators are the future of drivers' education programs. They are just one example of how virtual reality is influencing training and education.

perfect their driving skills from the safety of a classroom. VR programs like Aceable's Drivers Ed smartphone app are becoming popular teaching tools because they are effective and also make learning fun. Aceable's CEO and founder, Blake Garret, believes VR technology is a valuable teaching tool because it creates an active learning experience. "If you ask people about their best or most memorable learning experiences, they'll likely speak of learning something by playing a game or by practicing a skill in real life," Garret says.[3] Studies have shown that virtual reality experiences successfully cement lessons in people's memories.

EXPANDING APPLICATIONS

Driver education is just one area seeing the positive impacts of virtual reality. Many industries are embracing VR. For example, virtual reality has become a popular form of entertainment. VR action-adventure games such as Polyarc Inc.'s *Moss* draw players into fantasy worlds. Movie studios are starting to incorporate VR, too.

In December 2017, Paramount Studios and Bigscreen, a virtual reality platform, joined forces to bring the movie *Top Gun* into the Bigscreen virtual theater. For one day, viewers could choose from several showtimes and watch *Top Gun* for free. To participate in the event, users needed a VR headset and a computer with Windows 10 and Bigscreen's free program downloaded. Viewers virtually entered the Bigscreen lobby, which resembled a real theater. It had virtual concession booths, ticketing areas, and movie posters. Virtual moviegoers then watched *Top Gun* on a giant screen. In this way, VR allows people to share a movie experience even though they are not physically together. It also makes the movie theater experience accessible for people who cannot physically get to a theater. "Bigscreen's virtual reality platform offers a new way for fans to experience films in their homes. We're excited to be a part of this experiment using cutting-edge technology to give fans a new entertainment option," says Bob Buchi, Paramount's president of worldwide home media distribution.[4]

Several other industries are adding VR components to enhance training, manufacturing, education, and other experiences. VR's appeal lies in its ability to turn passive viewers into active participants. In education and training, VR scenarios can be repeated multiple times to reinforce training and ensure that the learner has confidently mastered the necessary skills. Some professional football players practice game plans while wearing VR headsets. VR is also a valuable tool for training professional drivers and pilots to safely operate vehicles. Delivery drivers can practice avoiding road hazards in VR before they get behind the wheel of a truck. Pilots can learn to navigate panels of complex controls in a virtual cockpit. They practice handling dangerous situations and performing tricky maneuvers in a safe environment. VR has been used by commercial and military pilots for training. Additionally, combat soldiers can safely practice military exercises in virtual reality. VR is also taking on a larger role in training medical professionals. With VR, surgeons can perfect techniques on virtual patients, eliminating the risk of injuring actual patients.

THE FUTURE OF VIRTUAL REALITY

Virtual reality has an exciting future. VR technology is no longer confined to research facilities or corporations—it's now accessible for many consumers. For example, VR arcades are popping up in malls and other venues in the United States and abroad. These arcades offer people of all ages a chance to experience VR without having to buy special equipment. VR's growth in the consumer market is expected to accelerate as the technology develops and prices decrease. In the meantime, more businesses are continuing to adopt VR. Large technology companies such as Facebook, Google, and Samsung are massively investing in developing VR hardware and software. Market research data collector Orbis Research predicts that the global virtual reality market could surpass $40 billion by 2020.

The more comfortable people are with VR, the more likely they are to incorporate the technology into their lives. In his January 2018 book *Experience on Demand*, Stanford University VR expert Jeremy Bailenson described VR's growth and the major impact the technology will have on society. He wrote, "Consumer VR is coming

Many companies are developing virtual reality technology, including Samsung, which made this headset. Facebook and Google are also investing in VR.

like a freight train. It may take two years, it may take ten, but mass adoption of affordable and powerful VR technology, combined with vigorous investment in content, is going to unleash a torrent of applications that will touch every aspect of our lives."[5]

While virtual reality has offered new opportunities in education, entertainment, and more, experts warn that there are downsides to the technology that should not be ignored. Like all technologies, there is potential for VR to be used in harmful ways. Experts warn that VR may be detrimental to people's psychological, social, and physical well-being. Virtual reality technology is still in its infancy, and experts acknowledge that VR could have undesirable side effects that may not be apparent for years to come. Even so, VR technology is advancing and increasingly becoming a part of everyday life.

What Is the Technology behind Virtual Reality?

T he key to virtual reality is computer technology that generates a three-dimensional environment capable of tricking a person's brain. People perceive the world around them through their five senses: sight, sound, smell, taste, and touch. The human sensory system involves complex interactions between the senses. When a person holds an object, it may feel cold, smooth, and heavy. Maybe the object vibrates, makes a loud noise, or has a distinct smell. Senses allow humans to feel temperature, texture, and many other signals from their environment. The information is relayed to the brain. Then the brain interprets the information, causing the body to react. When a cool breeze blows, a person shivers. When a door slams, people turn and look in the direction of the noise.

A great deal of what humans perceive is transmitted by sight. The separation between eyes on a human face is crucial to giving people a 3D perspective of the world. When a person looks at an object, the separation causes each eye to take in a slightly different view. Each image is transmitted to the brain, which then combines the information into a single image. Fusing the two perspectives creates a sense of depth. This is called **stereoscopic** vision.

Stereoscopic vision is critical to virtual reality. Virtual reality technology fools the brain by creating a realistic virtual 3D environment filled with sensory experiences. This feat is accomplished using a combination of computer software and hardware. With a virtual reality headset, powerful computer graphics output images that are displayed through two screens, one for each eye, to produce a 3D effect. The 3D image moves smoothly, reacting in real time to the movements of the user.

Additional hardware such as headsets, headphones, body sensors, and specialized gloves enhance the VR experience by adding the ability for users to interact with objects in the virtual world. In VR, a person can explore virtual environments that simulate real or fantasy settings. Users can drive cars or tour houses. They can explore Hawaiian volcanoes or the surface of Mars.

CREATING PRESENCE AND IMMERSION IN VIRTUAL WORLDS

The term *presence* describes the feeling a virtual reality user gets when he or she is immersed in the virtual environment. The virtual world feels physically real. As the user moves around the virtual environment, the VR technology system stimulates the user's senses in a way that corresponds to visual cues. The headset and other hardware, such as VR gloves or hand controls, contain sensors that track the user's hand and head movements. This tracking helps the technology respond to users' movements smoothly, with minimal delays. Users can reach out to touch and grab objects in the virtual environment. Accessories such as gloves and controllers can make these actions feel real by providing **haptic** feedback to the VR user. All of this enhances the realistic feeling of the virtual reality experience.

Daniel Newman, a researcher and writer, recounted in *Forbes* magazine his experience with virtual reality. "It's only a matter of seconds before you become completely entrenched in your new reality; looking, reaching, touching and experiencing an explosion of the senses," Newman wrote.[6] For VR users' presence to be the effective experience that Newman describes, they must be unable to detect any delay between when they move and when the VR environment responds. Any lag time that does occur is called latency. Latency prevents a user from being fully immersed in the VR world.

THE UPS AND DOWNS OF VR TECHNOLOGY

As modern virtual reality began to emerge in the 1980s, developers were met with many challenges. Limited computer capabilities combined with clumsy hardware and high costs kept virtual reality from becoming mainstream. "In the old days you would need six computers, but now all you need is one graphics card," says Rab Scott, a VR expert at the Nuclear Advanced Manufacturing Research Centre in England.[7] Advancements in computer technology have brought down costs and created user-friendly hardware components.

Virtual reality relies on a combination of software and hardware. VR content is designed on computers using modeling software programs. With additional software, the content is then displayed in a headset for a VR user to see. Devices such as a computer mouse, VR gloves, and controllers enable the user to interact with the VR environment.

Many inventions created as far back as the 1800s influenced the development of today's virtual reality systems. These include stereoscopic viewers, mechanical simulators, innovative film techniques, and various computer technologies. New devices and technologies continue to be developed, advancing the quality of the virtual reality experience.

EARLY VIEWERS AND SIMULATORS

Stereoscopic photo viewers were some of the earliest experiments that influenced the virtual reality headsets of today. In 1838, British physicist Charles Wheatstone presented an invention he called the stereoscope. The device used two mirrors to reflect slightly different images of the same scene into the observer's left and right eyes. The observer's eyes would blend the images into one view, which would be interpreted as 3D by the brain. Eleven years later, Scottish scientist and inventor David Brewster developed an improved portable stereoscope. His stereo camera fitted with two lenses could take two separate photos of the same scene. The photos were placed next to each other a set distance from the stereoscope viewing lenses. When viewers looked through lenses, they saw a 3D image.

In the 1950s, cinematographer Morton Heilig created an early simulator he called Sensorama. It immersed movie viewers in the film experience by stimulating all of their senses. The booth-like machine included a seat that faced a screen covered by a hood. For twenty-five cents, viewers could lean into the Sensorama to watch a two-minute 3D, full-color film. As they watched, viewers experienced stereo sound, vibrations, and smells that matched the movie's action and scenes. Heilig also invented a 3D camera and projector that he used

Stereoscopic viewers, like this one, are among early technologies that influenced virtual reality. But this stereoscope is much simpler than VR products available today.

to produce the five Sensorama films. In one film, *Motorcycle*, viewers took a multisensory motorcycle ride through the streets of New York City. The viewer's seat bounced and handlebars shook, just as they would on a real motorcycle ride. Engine and traffic sounds filled the booth as a fan blew a breeze in the viewer's face. Vents emitted the scent of exhaust. In 1962, Heilig described Sensorama as more than just an entertainment center. He believed the machine's true potential was as a tool for education and training. He said:

> *A basic concept in teaching is that a person will have a greater efficiency of learning if he can actually experience a situation as compared with merely reading about it or listening to a lecture. . . . If a student can experience a situation or an idea in about the same way that he experiences everyday life, it has been shown that he understands better and quicker.*[8]

Heilig went on to explain how adding stereo sound, scents, and other sensations created a feeling of reality for the viewer. However, Heilig was never able to secure investors and make the Sensorama a commercial success.

In 1961, engineers at Philco Corporation in Pennsylvania developed head-mounted displays (HMDs) that could track motion. This technology has also influenced modern virtual reality. Philco's HMD, called Headsight, was intended for helicopter pilots who flew at night. Headsight was a helmet with a video screen in front of each eye. A magnetic motion tracking system in the helmet was linked to a closed-circuit camera that would move as the wearer moved his head. The Headsight helmet allowed military pilots to remotely view dangerous areas.

The work of researchers exploring 3D interactive graphics during the 1960s and 1970s established the foundation for today's virtual reality technology. One such researcher was computer scientist Ivan Sutherland, who invented a computer program called Sketchpad in 1963. The revolutionary program allowed users to draw directly on a computer screen with a light pen. In his 1965 essay "The Ultimate Display," Sutherland revealed his ideas about the future capabilities of computer displays. Sutherland wrote:

> The ultimate display would, of course, be a room within which the computer can control the existence of matter. A chair displayed in such a room would be good enough to sit in. Handcuffs displayed in such a room would be confining, and a bullet displayed in such a room would be fatal. With appropriate programming, such a display could literally be the Wonderland into which Alice walked.[9]

He believed computer displays would eventually be used to access virtual worlds. Modern VR technology is getting closer and closer to Sutherland's predictions.

One of Sutherland's major contributions to VR occurred in 1968 when he and student Bob Sproull created an HMD and connected it to a computer instead of a camera. The computer generated simple 3D **wireframe** images such as cubes. Considered the first true virtual reality HMD, Sutherland's invention was so heavy it had to hang from a mechanical arm attached to the ceiling. The HMD was called the Sword of Damocles after the ancient Greek parable in which a sword is suspended from the ceiling above a man's head by a single horsehair. Sutherland's HMD had a sensor that tracked the wearer's head movements. The sensor established where the wearer was looking. Through the HMD, a viewer entered a simple computer-generated wireframe room and looked around the room by turning his head. Years later, at a VR technology awards ceremony, Sutherland explained what made his HMD different than earlier inventions. "My little contribution to virtual reality was to realize that we didn't need a camera. We could substitute a computer. . . . It was quite a crude thing. It was not real in any sense. But it was three-dimensional," he said.[10] Sutherland's innovative research with head-mounted displays and 3D computer graphics gave momentum to research into virtual reality technology.

Another pioneer in the field of virtual reality was Jaron Lanier. In 1987, Lanier founded VPL Research, and he is credited with popularizing the term *virtual reality*. VPL researchers advanced virtual reality technology by developing and selling virtual reality software

> **WORDS IN CONTEXT**
>
> **wireframe**
> A simple, skeletal representation of an object, made of only lines.

VIRTUAL REALITY HEADSETS FOR CONSUMERS (2018)

Headset	Launch Price	Year Released
HTC Vive	$799	April 2016
Oculus Rift	$599	March 2016
Sony PlayStation VR	$399	October 2016
Google Daydream View	$99	November 2016
Samsung Gear VR	$99	November 2015
Google Cardboard	$20	June 2014

and hardware. VPL's products included the EyePhone head-mounted display, the DataGlove, and, later, the DataSuit. The EyePhone HMDs had low resolution, so scenes often appeared blurry. The DataGlove contained fiber-optic sensors that allowed a computer to track finger flexing and hand movements. With the DataGlove, a person could manipulate 3D computer-generated objects. But DataGloves had problems. They did not provide tactile feedback and did not fit well on different hand sizes. VPL's DataSuit was a full-body system that tracked people's movements to enhance their VR experiences. All of VPL's products had high price tags, costing thousands of dollars.

The 1990s experienced a surge of virtual reality technology, primarily for video games. A range of VR headsets, 3D gaming consoles, and other virtual reality software and hardware products were released. Popular movies featured fictional, futuristic VR, which created public excitement about experiencing virtual worlds. "Virtual reality got featured in movies, TV shows, games, and books as a kind of holy grail technology about to change the world," said Palmer Luckey, a VR entrepreneur and inventor.[11] Despite the hype and an onslaught of new products, VR did not immediately catch on with consumers. The promising technology was fraught with problems. Hardware was clunky and expensive. Computer processing power was inadequate, and graphics were unrealistic. VR kits like Nintendo's Virtual Boy game console and headset, which went on sale for $180 in 1994, had limited capabilities. The console featured only red and black graphics, rather than full color. It also lacked motion tracking capability, which caused users to get headaches. Virtual Boy and many similar VR gaming products failed because they did not meet consumer expectations. After a long string of failures, the business of virtual reality cooled off until 2012, when inventor Luckey introduced the world to his VR headset, Oculus Rift.

Oculus Rift created one of the first modern virtual reality systems. Several other inventions led to today's VR technology.

MODERN VIRTUAL REALITY HARDWARE

Early hardware developed for VR systems was clumsy and difficult to use. But today's powerful computer processors, sharp display technology, and advanced sensors have resulted in an array of VR hardware devices that are small, powerful, and easy to use. Headsets can be made of cardboard, plastic, fabric, and metal. Liquid crystal display (LCD) screens in front of each eye create a sense of depth for the viewer. HMDs are designed to keep the display in front of users' eyes no matter which way they turn their heads. Most HMDs also contain speakers or headphones for sound. Tracking devices embedded in HMDs have sensors that follow the viewer's head movements. They relay head movement and positioning information

PRACTICE MAKES PERFECT

Virtual reality software creates scenarios within which users can practice a task as many times as required in order to master skills. Many colleges now rely on virtual reality software to help their sports teams prepare for games. Athletes can use VR to practice at any time without being on a field. Dartmouth College football team head coach Buddy Teevens has said virtual reality plays an important part in the team's success. "The wonderful benefit . . . is that you can take an exponential number of visual snaps without being on the field or having to go through a practice format. A guy does a limited amount of work on the field, but he can double, triple, quadruple that sitting in his dormitory, the study lounge, or the video library." An added benefit is that virtual training doesn't require physical contact, so it also helps cut down on injuries. Many large corporations also use virtual reality to train their employees. At Walmart training centers, new hires wear HMDs to learn customer service skills. They also practice for difficult situations, such as the rush of shoppers the day after Thanksgiving in the United States.

Quoted in Justin Kramer, "Football Team Uses State-of-the-Art Virtual Reality Tool," *The Dartmouth*, February 9, 2018. www.thedartmouth.com.

also contain speakers or headphones for sound. Tracking devices embedded in HMDs have sensors that follow the viewer's head movements. They relay head movement and positioning information to the computer processor. The processor sends images back to the HMD display that correspond with where the viewer is looking. Some HMDs do not contain computing power and must be tethered to computers or game consoles by cables. Other HMDs are mobile and use a smartphone for processing power and the display. Other devices such as hand controllers provide users with a more immersive experience. Hand controllers provide haptic feedback that allows users to touch and feel objects in VR.

mobile headsets such as Google Cardboard, Google Daydream View, and Samsung Gear VR. Tethered HMDs are more expensive and cumbersome, but they provide a richer, more complex VR experience with detailed images, motion sensing, and superior tracking. Inexpensive mobile headsets cannot deliver the same resolution and sense stimulation. But they are an affordable, easy-to-use option.

TETHERED HEADSETS

Luckey arrived on the VR scene in 2012 when he began a Kickstarter crowdfunding campaign to raise money for the development of his VR headset, which he called Oculus Rift. Hoping to raise $250,000 to produce a few hundred headsets, Luckey instead received $2.5 million. In 2014, Facebook founder Mark Zuckerberg was so interested in the new VR headset that he bought Luckey's company for $2 billion. Oculus Rift HMDs went on sale on March 28, 2016. The headset was lightweight and comfortable. It delivered crisp, clear graphics for playing immersive games. It cost about $600. While the original Oculus Rift could track head movements and was primarily for gaming, Zuckerberg believed future headsets would have expanded capabilities and uses. In a letter posted on Facebook in 2014, Zuckerberg stated, "After games, we're going to make Oculus a platform for many other experiences. Imagine enjoying a courtside seat at a game, studying in a classroom of students and teachers all over the world or consulting with a doctor face-to-face—just by putting on goggles in your home."[12] Additions to the original Oculus Rift headset include Oculus Touch motion controllers, which allow users to incorporate their natural hand gestures and movements into their VR experiences. VR units like Oculus Rift require a powerful—and expensive—computer to run properly. Popular Oculus Rift games include Lone Echo, Elite: Dangerous, and Star Trek: Bridge Crew. As of early 2018, the Oculus Rift headset was one of the top-selling

Google Cardboard is meant to provide an affordable way for people to experience virtual reality. It operates with a smartphone.

VR HMDs, grabbing 46 percent of the market. Other tethered VR sets include the Sony PlayStation VR and HTC Vive. The PlayStation VR runs on the PlayStation 4 console, rather than on an expensive gaming PC. This makes it cheaper and more accessible to a wider audience. The HTC Vive uses a tracking technology that enables "room scale" VR. Room scale allows users to move through a larger 3D space than they can with other headsets. Like Oculus Rift, these headsets are for gaming. Additional accessories such as motion controllers and base stations enhance the VR experience. Base stations are devices that provide a smoother VR experience by tracking the exact locations of headsets and controllers as users move around.

GOOGLE'S MOBILE VR DEVICES

Google Cardboard is the simplest VR headset. Released in 2014, it lets anyone with a smartphone experience VR. It is made from folded cardboard pieces, magnets, and two lenses. Anyone can assemble the lightweight goggles in a matter of minutes. Then a smartphone is inserted into the headset, which the user holds up to his or her face. Google has produced several smartphone apps that create the VR experience.

Mobile VR devices take advantage of the technologies already built into every smartphone. A sharp display allows phone users to use apps and read text easily. When used for VR, the clarity of the display helps to create an immersive world. Motion sensors in phones tell the display to rotate when the user turns the phone sideways. When used for VR, these sensors can calculate the user's head movements. Cardboard viewers sell for as little as $15. Google Cardboard's popularity is evident in its sales numbers. Since 2014, more than 10 million headsets have been sold. In 2016, Google introduced a more upscale VR mobile headset called Google Daydream View. Unlike the Cardboard, the Google Daydream View is a sturdy, fabric-covered device. A front panel folds down so users can insert a compatible smartphone.

How Does Virtual Reality Positively Impact Society?

As the cost of VR hardware declines, virtual reality technology is becoming more accessible and slowly spreading into more areas of daily life. Many organizations are venturing into VR and realizing the benefits of this new technology. Studies show that VR engages students and improves information retention. Businesses and the military use VR to train their personnel. Architects, engineers, and other professionals are discovering innovative applications for VR, using the technology to design and sell products. Health care professionals practice surgical techniques and ease patient anxiety with virtual reality applications. VR in the entertainment industry is expanding beyond gaming into movies and new ways of socializing. Virtual reality offers a seemingly endless supply of potential uses.

VR IN THE CLASSROOM

Novi Woods Elementary School teacher Michelle Donberger and her class regularly travel the world together without ever leaving their Michigan classroom. On an underwater expedition, they navigated coral reefs and swam with hammerhead sharks. During a history lesson, Donberger and her students traveled back in time to an American pioneers' settlement, complete with a covered wagon. The virtual reality app Google Expeditions, along with Google Cardboard viewers, makes these trips come to life. The teacher guides her

Elementary school teachers are starting to use virtual reality in the classroom. Many children this age are already comfortable using computers, smartphones, and other technology.

students through the field trip using an app downloaded to her iPad. Educators may buy a kit containing the needed hardware from Google, or they can make their own. Kits include a tablet for the teacher, smartphones with the Expeditions app, and Google Cardboard viewers for the students. Many schools, including Novi Woods Elementary School, collect donated iPhones. Schools with no access to the Internet can still use Expeditions by loading lessons onto the teacher's tablet. The teacher uses the tablet to control how the class moves through the VR experience. A guide provided by Google helps teachers highlight key elements as students move

Teachers say virtual reality helps provide a more hands-on learning experience for students. However, the technology is not replacing standard teaching.

through the virtual experience. "You can guide kids like it's a field trip. Arrows show up, like, 'Look over here, there is a hammerhead shark, this is what it's known for and what they eat.' It's very simple," says Donberger.[13] Students are already comfortable using technology such as smartphones and tablets, so they quickly adapt to the Cardboard viewers.

Virtual field trips and other uses of VR are becoming valuable teaching tools. Teachers, however, emphasize that VR is not replacing traditional teaching methods. Instead, they see VR as a powerful tool for engaging students and enhancing learning by providing experiences that would otherwise not be possible. Marietta Leon, who teaches with Donberger, explains, "It's a great extension of what we're talking about in class. You can read books, but with the Google Expedition, it's kind of like you're there getting that hands-on experience . . . being able to see some of the animals you couldn't see at the zoo, being able to go to places that you would never get to go."[14] Expeditions programs are flexible and can be adapted to any lesson plan or age level. "The imagery is the same, what changes is the particular engagement of the teacher. We wanted it to be super flexible," says Jennifer Holland, an education program manager at Google.[15] A VR experience in the Great Barrier Reef works for discussing animal interactions with third graders or for explaining how climate change affects coral to middle schoolers. VR experiences cover all curriculum topics from math to science to history.

In January 2018, Google for Education launched a program that takes Google Expeditions one step further. The new program gives teachers and students the opportunity to create their own virtual expeditions. Educators and students use a 360-degree camera to create a 360-degree image. Once the image is uploaded to the Google app, students can add descriptions, 2D pictures and videos. "A 'create-your-own' experience is the top feature that teachers and students wanted in Google Expeditions," Holland says.[16] The program is still in the testing phase, but it already allows students to work together, share expeditions, and be creative. Many teachers are adding virtual reality components into their curricula. The interactive nature of VR engages students. The hands-on VR experience helps students understand and retain the information presented. VR's flexibility lets educators customize lessons.

VR ENHANCES MUSEUMS

Many museums are incorporating virtual reality into their exhibits and programs to support their missions while making exhibits active and engaging for visitors. At the Jewish Museum in New York, a 2016 exhibit showcased the work of French furniture designer Pierre Chareau. The exhibit galleries of his pieces were equipped with virtual reality gear. With headsets on, visitors were transported to the Maison de Verre (House of Glass) in Paris and 1920s-era apartments decorated with Chareau's furniture. Exhibit designers turned to virtual reality so that visitors could see how Chareau's pieces looked in their original settings. "These solo pieces are meaningful in their native settings, but removed they lose their relationship to space, to architecture, to time, to function. . . . Virtual reality provided the perfect opportunity to re-spatialize these artifacts, these pieces of furniture," says Elizabeth Diller, an architect who worked on the exhibit.[17]

In 2016, the Smithsonian American Art Museum (SAAM) in Washington, DC, released its first VR mobile app. With the app, anyone can visit the WONDER exhibit at the museum's Renwick Gallery without going to the museum. Any VR headset, such as Google Cardboard, can be used with the app. The WONDER exhibit features art installations by nine artists. During the virtual tour, app users can access extra features, such as video interviews with the artists. "The museum has always embraced new technologies to bring our collection to people wherever they are. We're excited to use the latest virtual reality technology to add a new dimension to the museum experience," says Betsy Broun of SAAM.[18] Virtual museum tours and specialized apps are making museums accessible to people all over the world.

It's less expensive for engineers to create virtual prototypes of cars instead of building physical prototypes. In this way, virtual reality technology could improve manufacturing practices.

BUSINESS APPLICATIONS OF VR

Engineering, construction, and architecture are all reaping the benefits of VR technology. Virtual prototypes can be analyzed for design and safety issues before physical products are made, saving time and money. Virtual reality has been a part of the car design and manufacturing processes at Ford Motor Company's facility in Dearborn, Michigan, since 2013. Designers, engineers, and other specialists wear Oculus Rift or HTC Vive headsets. Virtual reality is used to design, develop, and test new vehicles before manufacturing even begins.

Virtual reality can help companies sell cars. The technology can be used to show vehicles to customers.

Car companies such as Ford that have adopted VR technology are making the switch from constructing physical car prototypes to building most models with virtual reality. Virtual car prototypes are easy to alter early in the design process so cars can enter the production phase faster. "The impact on cost, time, and quality are significant and have allowed our designers and engineers more creative freedoms to explore options that in the past would have been too time- or cost-intensive to consider," says Ford technical leader Jeff Greenberg.[19] Ford was the first automaker to use ultrahigh-definition VR that permits designers and engineers at Ford facilities around the world to collaborate on projects. At the Ford Immersive Vehicle

Environment (FIVE) Lab, designers review virtual vehicles to ensure that they meet quality and comfort standards.

Virtual reality applications are ideal for architects. Architects can use VR technology to create and modify designs before any construction happens. Sometimes architects enter spaces they have designed only to realize that the building isn't quite what they had envisioned. "More often than not, I'll go to my own projects and be like, 'Wow! That's a lot bigger than I expected,'" says Hao Ko of Gensler, an architectural and design firm.[20] Just as engineers from Ford's FIVE Lab collaborate on projects, architects connect with each other and with clients in 3D virtual spaces through multi-user VR. The technology is also a convenient and flexible way for architects to showcase and share their work portfolio with clients. While wearing headsets, designers and clients can virtually explore a space. They get a physical feel for the space in a way that's not possible from simply looking at architectural drawings. "We just had a client where we were showing some conceptual renderings, and they were having a hard time [understanding the building]. The second we put goggles on them, it was like, 'Oh yeah. Build that. That's great. That's what I want,'" says Ko.[21] During a virtual walk-through, designers and clients interact and customize details on the spot. Construction and design issues can be identified and taken care of before construction begins. Employing VR technology in the design phase avoids costly post-construction alterations and helps firms anticipate the need for special equipment or process steps. It also eliminates the cost of flights and meeting expenses associated with bringing designers and clients together to a site. ZGF Architects used VR in their design of the F5 Tower, a skyscraper in Seattle, Washington. A VR walk-through of the building helped ZGF's client decide to choose marble floors for the lobby. "We needed a way to make quick, informed decisions between the architects, interior designers, all the way to the head of security, who would be posted in the lobby. It's a great tool for communicating to everybody, whether they understand architectural drawings or not," says Simon Manning of ZGF.[22] More architecture firms are incorporating virtual reality to stay competitive.

VIRTUAL REALITY SELLS PRODUCTS

Not only does virtual reality help businesses create better products—it also serves as a powerful marketing tool. Customers who see, feel, and use products in VR may be more apt to make a purchase. Virtual reality can also build customer excitement about products before they are released. When carmaker Volvo wanted potential buyers to know about its new XC90 SUV, it produced a VR test drive app for smartphones and Google Cardboard. The VR experience was released months before the car was available in showrooms. Bodil Eriksson of Volvo explains what the app does: "What we have done is to create a virtual reality test drive allowing consumers to join us for, in all, three episodes of the all new XC90 test drive. . . . You feel absolutely like you're in the car."[23] As viewers travel the countryside in the XC90, they can evaluate the car and decide if it's right for them.

Retail stores are also investing in VR experiences with the hope of attracting and retaining customers. In 2017, the home improvement company Lowe's made virtual reality part of the shopping experience at some of its stores. The "Holoroom How To" is a do-it-yourself virtual clinic produced by Lowe's Innovation Labs. Every year, people begin home improvement projects but fail to complete them. This happens because people often lack the confidence or knowledge to finish a task, according to the creators of Holoroom How To. "People learn by doing. It's just how we are built. And that's why we built the Holoroom How To. The Holoroom How To is a virtual reality training tool that teaches people how to do DIY projects . . . anything from painting a fence to tiling a bathroom," says Kyle Nel of Lowe's Innovation Labs.[24] Inside the Holoroom booth, customers can wear an Oculus Rift headset and use a hand controller to retile a bathroom wall. With the haptic controller, customers can feel as though they are smoothing grout or pressing tiles in place. They get a chance to practice the skills necessary to tackle an actual remodeling project. Nel emphasizes that consumers learn skills more effectively when they use VR to learn in the Holoroom. "[We did a] test and half the customers went through the virtual reality Holoroom How To and the other half just watched

VIRTUAL REALITY SELLS REAL ESTATE

Virtual reality is changing the way people buy real estate. By wearing a headset, buyers can tour properties from the real estate office without having to travel. "You could have a buyer anywhere—in the Hamptons or California or Colorado or London—and they can receive a link, put on their Google Cardboard, and then be right in the middle of the room or the house," says real estate broker Paul Hyun. Some of the hardest real estate to sell is property that has not yet been developed or is partially completed. Many buyers are not willing to take a risk on property that exists only in plans on paper. But with virtual reality, prospective buyers can tour properties even before they have been constructed. Vitre is a forty-eight-unit condo building planned for Manhattan's Upper East Side. After taking a virtual tour, one couple purchased a penthouse unit even though it wouldn't be ready until later that year. "The reality is, a lot of real estate is emotional. [With VR], you can actually walk around the unit and take into account the floor plan and views and stuff you wouldn't be able to see in any sales center mock-up or drawing," says buyer Amol Shah. Some large real estate developers are finding virtual reality tours so efficient and effective that they are hiring dedicated VR teams to create tours for their properties.

Quoted in Adam Bonislawski, "Brokers Are Using Virtual Reality Headsets to Sell Apartments," *New York Post*, November 29, 2017. www.nypost.com.

a YouTube video. Customers who went through the virtual reality version had 36 percent better recall," Nel says.[25] Customers who feel confident about their skills are more apt to buy materials and complete their DIY projects, he said.

JOB TRAINING THROUGH VIRTUAL REALITY

Virtual reality provides a safe environment for companies to train people for jobs, especially potentially hazardous jobs. NextWave is a VR technology company that makes training programs for construction companies and other organizations such as the New York City Fire Department. Two of NextWave's VR modules are called "Hazard ID" and "Forklift." During the Hazard ID session, employees wear an HTC Vive headset while they identify hazards on a construction site. Users click on exposed electrical wires or improperly covered manhole covers, and then they answer questions about proper safety techniques. The Forklift training module uses a VR headset, handle controllers, and foot pedals. Users navigate through a warehouse and learn to operate a forklift. Gary Foreman, chief technology officer at NextWave, says the immersive nature of VR training improves retention. "We're trying to make these experiences as accurate as possible so it's not replacing existing training but adding another dimension. Current OSHA [Occupational Safety and Health Administration] classes are not compelling. You're sitting there looking at old PowerPoints and videos. VR can change all of that," he explains.[26]

An added benefit is that training sessions can be recorded to ensure that trainees master the needed skills. Foreman says:

We can measure and monitor every action—every button press, every turn, where they go within an environment—to track whether

*the user actually understands what they're being taught. Because
it's VR, we can do things in a safer environment that doesn't
disrupt the real-world production of a warehouse or a construction
site. Ultimately, the goal is to create much better training so there
are fewer accidents to workers and the people around them.*[27]

In some jobs, potential employees need more than physical skills.
Workers in high-risk jobs must also be psychologically prepared to
handle the stress. "Just because you pass a permit test doesn't mean
you know how to drive a car. I can't tell you how many times we had
someone take a scaffolding course and passed it, and then they went
23 stories up and froze in fear and we had to call EMS [emergency
medical services] and the fire department," says NextWave CEO
Lorenzo Gallo, who also runs a safety training company.[28] Gallo says
that this type of reaction prevents work from continuing and can put
other workers in danger. By providing more realistic training scenarios,
virtual reality can help identify people who may not be able to handle
the stress of a job.

MEETING VIRTUALLY

Meetings are needed in any business, but they can be costly and time
consuming. In 2017, business travel spending in the United States
reached $304.9 billion. While businesses have been using video
conferencing for years, many employees feel it limits interaction. They
are sometimes unable to see each
other's hand gestures and facial
expressions. Virtual reality brings a
whole new dimension to meetings.
At a VR conference, employees see
digital **avatars** of themselves in a
simulated environment. Through the

WORDS IN CONTEXT

avatar
A virtual icon that represents
a person.

avatars, attendees can move around, look at each other, share documents, and even create 3D models together. "VR meetings will allow for nuanced nonverbal communication—proper eye contact, subtle cues such as interpersonal distance, and eventually virtual touch and smell," VR expert Jeremy Bailenson says.[29] VR conferencing is also valuable for employees who work remotely. They would be able to meet and interact with other workers at their company.

MILITARY BENEFITS FROM VR

The US military has been developing and using virtual reality technologies since the 1920s and 1930s. In fact, both the navy and air force were involved in the early development of HMDs. Today, all five branches of the US military—army, navy, air force, marines, and coast guard—apply virtual reality in training, maneuver analysis, and personnel recruitment. Training military personnel is costly, time consuming, and often dangerous. Virtual reality applications offer an effective, efficient, and safe way to prepare military personnel. Simulators train military pilots as well as soldiers who operate military vehicles such as tanks and submarines. VR provides a safe environment for soldiers to practice skills and battlefield tactics. VR scenarios are customizable, so soldiers can train for combat in specific regions. This way, when they arrive in a region, soldiers will be familiar with the terrain and better equipped to navigate their surroundings. VR also allows trainees to work together even though they may be located far from each other. Incoming military personnel have grown up with digital equipment and are typically comfortable using virtual reality.

Flight simulators are designed to replicate the look and feel of real aircraft cockpits. They provide haptic feedback to trainees as they

The military has been developing virtual reality technology, including flight simulators, for many years. But these flight simulators are no longer just for military pilots; consumers can experience flying through virtual reality as well.

manipulate cockpit controls and perfect their flying skills. Pilots sit on a hydraulic lift system or an electronic motion base that moves with the pilot and reacts to the simulation. The simulators are programmed to respond accurately to the pilot's input. Users can learn cockpit procedures and practice maneuvers in a safe environment. Even after learning to fly, pilots refresh their skills in simulators. Virtual reality flying simulations place pilots in realistic combat scenarios. New improvements to VR technology produce more realistic and customizable situations and reduce unpleasant VR side effects such as nausea and headaches.

Another type of simulator immerses soldiers in combat missions. The Dismounted Soldier Training System (DSTS) includes a full range of training environments such as mountains, woods, and deserts. These are common locations that soldiers might find themselves in while on a real-life mission. Trainees suit up with virtual reality HMD helmets, armor, and replica rifles. A computer pack on each soldier's back transmits images to the HMD. Sensors track the soldier's motions. During training with the DSTS, soldiers practice different combat scenarios involving firefights with enemies. "The DSTS teaches you how to make the decision to fire. It's okay for you to mess up in here, because this is a simulator. If you mess up out there, it's not okay," says specialist Josh Miller of the 11th Combat Aviation Brigade.[30] DSTS simulators can also connect with flight simulators in other rooms to create a more integrated simulation. During these combined virtual reality exercises, soldiers on the ground can practice working together with military aircraft soaring overhead. Training sessions are recorded so soldiers receive feedback on their performance. Soldiers can repeat DSTS sessions to experience different battles and perfect their skills.

Military use of VR training has other benefits as well. Reducing the need to train in real-life settings saves lives. In October 2014 alone, there were three crashes involving military aircraft in combat and training exercises. Two pilots in these incidents were injured, and another was killed. Pilots can safely practice dangerous flight maneuvers and skills such as parachute jumps in VR. Integrating live and simulated training also cuts costs. Using simulators and other VR exercises means less money is spent on maintaining aircraft and other vehicles. It also reduces the monetary costs of trainees' errors. Also, coordinating exercises in VR is far less expensive than physically bringing together trainees and equipment from different locations.

MEDICAL APPLICATIONS FOR VR

Virtual reality is having a major impact in the field of medicine. Dr. David Axelrod of Stanford University is a pediatric cardiologist who virtually walks inside his patients' hearts. Axelrod partnered with David Sarno, founder of Lighthaus, a company that creates virtual content, to create the Stanford Virtual Heart. This application takes doctors into virtual hearts so they can observe **congenital** defects. These structural heart defects are complex and varied, which makes them challenging to understand. Medical professionals often struggle to explain heart defects to students and patients' families with plastic models and diagrams. Using the Stanford Virtual Heart, viewers can enter and move around a beating heart. During the experience, participants observe how the organ works and how blood flows. By being immersed in the heart, viewers get a better grasp of how the defective heart compares with a normal heart. Axelrod says:

> Our virtual heart goes so far beyond what textbooks, plastic models, and even **cadavers** have taught medical trainees for decades. It gives them a vivid three-dimensional sense of how the heart works and what happens when it's not working normally. This is just a better way to teach our medical trainees, doctors, nurses, and even families about complex anatomy that they've never seen before.[31]

Similar virtual experiences are being developed, changing the future of medical training. VR helps medical staff grasp issues faster and more thoroughly. The result is quicker patient diagnosis and more

Virtual reality exposure therapy has proven to be effective for people suffering from post-traumatic stress disorder. This therapy has been used by soldiers and veterans.

effective treatment. Doctors and nurses are also using VR applications to practice surgeries. VR is a safe environment to try out new techniques and to hone skills without risking patients' lives.

Virtual reality technology is relieving pain and psychological stress as well. In Oakland, California, children being treated for sickle cell disease at the University of California San Francisco's Benioff Children's Hospital enter virtual worlds to find relief from their pain. Simon Robertson is the founder of KindVR, a company that makes custom VR software to help ease pain and stress from medical conditions. He visits patients at Benioff with a headset and takes them on VR adventures that distract them from their pain. Patients can scuba dive with whales and dolphins and discover sunken treasure. "It's not like your typical video game. It's soothing. It takes away all negativity," said one young patient named Briana.[32] Robertson agrees that the VR experiences have a positive impact on the patients he works with. "I've watched patients who can barely sit up and say hello to me put on the headset and feel energized and confident and able to move around and it's amazing to see that effect," Robertson says.[33] Virtual reality experiences diminish pain by giving the brain something else to focus on. Dr. Anne Marsh, who treats children with sickle cell disease, believes that VR experiences are valuable pain management tools. "I think that virtual reality technology has the potential to transform pain management," Marsh says.[34] Marsh hopes VR will eventually be used to treat other ailments as well.

Soldiers and others who experience traumatic events often suffer from post-traumatic stress disorder (PTSD). The disorder has a host of symptoms including nightmares, difficulty sleeping, guilt, and feeling isolated. The life-altering symptoms can last for years. PTSD patients often undergo exposure therapy, which has them confront their trauma by retelling their experience. Researchers have found that adding virtual reality experiences to exposure therapy effectively helps patients overcome PTSD. PTSD sufferers often avoid recalling their traumatic experience. Virtual reality exposure therapy (VRET) gives patients a way to confront their trauma by gradually immersing them in virtual scenarios that simulate their traumatic experience. Bravemind is a VRET application developed by the University of Southern California Institute for Creative Technologies. The software can be tailored to meet the needs of each patient. A trained therapist controls the virtual experience, which includes sound, vibrations, and even smells to stimulate the patient's senses. Therapists can monitor and record patient responses. In addition to helping treat PTSD patients, Bravemind has also become a tool for understanding the brain's reaction to trauma. With this information, doctors hope to find ways to prevent and treat PTSD more effectively.

Chapter 60

How Does Virtual Reality Negatively Impact Society?

T he virtual reality industry is still in the early stages of development, so not much is known about the negative impacts of using VR. However, experts have already noticed that virtual reality experiences have had some undesirable physical and **psychological** side effects. When consumers purchase VR equipment, they also receive information warning about them about the problems that can be caused by using virtual reality. These problems may be physical effects, including dizziness and nausea, that subside once the person takes off the VR headset. Other consequences include more serious reactions such as **seizures**. As more people spend time in virtual reality, researchers are finding that VR may also negatively affect human behavior. VR experiences can cause a range of psychological issues, including trauma, obsession, and isolation. There are also privacy concerns surrounding VR technology. Experts warn that the VR industry needs more regulation to protect users' rights and privacy.

PHYSICAL SIDE EFFECTS

Consumer demand for virtual headsets such as Sony PlayStation VR, Oculus Rift, and HTC Vive is increasing, and prices are decreasing. During the third quarter of 2017, more than one million VR units were shipped worldwide. The increased number of headsets in use exposes more people to the potential hazards associated with virtual reality hardware and software. The most obvious concern is injury caused by distraction. VR users are essentially blind to their physical environments when they are wearing headsets. Many VR applications are operated while users sit or stand in place. But during room-scale VR, users move around in a space that they establish before beginning the VR experience. Despite setting up a cleared VR area, there have

been numerous instances of users hitting or running into walls, other objects, or people in the room. It's also possible to trip and fall over the cables connecting the headset and controllers to other equipment. In a tragic incident in Russia in 2017, a man died after he fell while wearing a VR headset. "According to preliminary information, the man tripped and crashed into a glass table, suffered wounds, and died on the spot from loss of blood," says Yulia Ivanova, an assistant of the Russian Investigative Committee.[35]

People with preexisting medical issues such as heart conditions, anxiety disorders, or PTSD may experience negative side effects from using virtual reality. While using VR with a trained therapist is valuable in helping people overcome PTSD and other psychological disorders, frightening VR experiences can trigger anxiety for anyone. It can be especially problematic for people with mental health conditions. Pregnant or elderly VR users are also at risk. Virtual reality events such as falling from great heights or being frightened by a scary character can be so realistic that users' bodies react as though the experiences are real. This can cause a user's heart rate and blood pressure to

Virtual reality can cause many physical side effects, including headaches. As the technology develops, researchers will learn more about these side effects.

increase, which is dangerous for people who are elderly, pregnant, or have heart conditions. A frightening scene in VR may cause real and lasting trauma. Additionally, people who are ill, extremely tired, or have ingested alcohol or drugs may become sicker after using VR. Some people, particularly children and teens, are naturally sensitive to flickering or flashing lights. The sensitivity, a condition known as photosensitive epilepsy, causes them to have seizures. Exposure to light patterns during virtual reality sessions may cause people with epilepsy to experience seizures, dizziness, and fainting. VR consumer health and safety information carries warnings about these and other harmful effects that VR can cause.

People with no preexisting illness can still suffer from a form of motion sickness called virtual reality sickness. VR makes some people nauseous and dizzy. Motion sickness occurs when the senses that help maintain balance conflict with each other. During a virtual reality experience, a person's eyes sense that he or she is in motion. In contrast, the person's inner ear, which plays a role in maintaining balance, senses that the person is stationary. This mismatch of information being transmitted to the brain can make people feel sick. Lag time between a user's actions and what he or she sees in VR also contributes to VR sickness. Professor John F. Golding of the University of Westminster in London is a scientist who specializes in motion sickness. He explains:

> As you move your head with a VR headset on, the advanced sensors in the headset will know you're moving and refresh the screen accordingly to make it move the right way—this ensures what you're seeing is as real as possible. . . . But, it can't do it as fast as it needs to in most cases. It needs to do it in 5 to 10 milliseconds, and if there's any kind of lag, it can cause sensory conflict, even it seems real enough to you consciously.[36]

Virtual reality may also negatively affect people's vision through a condition called vergence-accommodation conflict (VAC). While viewing images in virtual reality, a person is staring at a screen just inches from his or her face. But to see what is going on in the simulated world, the viewer must shift focus to images that appear farther away. Focusing issues are worse for people who are near- or far-sighted. VAC causes headaches, nausea, fatigue, and eye strain that may last even after people stop using the headset. Researchers are exploring new VR display designs to minimize or eliminate VAC. Some eye specialists believe that VR, like other screen technologies, will increase the number of people with **myopia** or nearsightedness. Studies show that there has been a substantial increase in people with nearsightedness, rising from 25 percent of the US population in the 1970s to more than 40 percent by 2000. "Looking at tablets, phones and the like, there's pretty good evidence that doing near work can cause lengthening of the eye and increase risk for myopia," says Dr. Martin Banks, an optometry professor at the University of California.[37] As more people use virtual reality at home, school, and work, cases of myopia and other eye problems may increase.

VR'S PSYCHOLOGICAL POWER

The feeling of presence that users experience during a virtual reality session is what makes virtual reality unique and powerful. But researchers are finding that the realistic experiences have the power to cause psychological trauma. They are examining how VR may negatively influence human behavior and morality. "VR experiences can be incredible and truly offer promising new ways to address societal problems. . . . But if a virtual experience is powerful enough to alter our fundamental views about the planet or race relations, then it must also have possibilities for ill [purposes]," VR expert Jeremy Bailenson says.[38]

One area that concerns researchers is how violence in virtual reality will influence people's real-life behavior. One study by researchers at Ohio State University found that people's anger significantly increased while playing violent video games with 3D glasses. Study participants played *Grand Theft Auto IV*, a game that has players engage in violent activities such as carjacking and robbery. After fifteen minutes, people who played in 3D felt angrier than people who played in 2D, without the 3D glasses. Professor Brad Bushman, who coauthored the study, says, "3D gaming increases anger because the players felt more immersed in the violence when they played violent games. As the technology in video games improves, it has the ability to have stronger effects on players."[39] Experts are concerned because virtual reality is far more realistic than any video game shown on a flat screen, including those played with 3D glasses. Controllers and sensors that provide haptic feedback create sensations that make VR gamers feel as though they are committing violent acts. The immersive feeling of performing violent acts in VR could increase player violence in real life and cause desensitization to violence. Even worse, violent VR worlds may also help people perfect violent skills such as shooting accuracy.

The realistic nature of virtual reality can make frightening VR games psychologically traumatizing for viewers. Positional tracking on headsets heightens fear by putting terrifying elements in the viewer's visual range in response to head movements. Jon Hibbins of Psytec Games explains how a monster in the game *Crystal Rift* reacts to the player's movements. "A monster can appear in a vent only when the player looks at the vent," he says.[40] By knowing where a viewer is looking, game producers enhance the scare factor. "With that knowledge, we can play mind tricks or trigger events based on the gaze," Hibbins says.[41] For some, the images might be too intense. Realistic VR experiences can form strong, long-lasting memories. "VR can be stored in the brain's memory center in ways that are strikingly similar to real-world physical experiences. When VR is done well, the brain believes it is real," Bailenson says.[42] Frightening VR content creates the same physical reactions that real frightening events do. Viewers can experience increased heart rate and blood pressure. The anxiety and fear may feel so real that it causes post-traumatic stress disorder. Researchers Michael Madary and Thomas K. Metzinger of the Johannes Gutenberg University in Germany have studied virtual reality and its psychological effects on humans. They found evidence that feelings and memories can linger after frightening or anxiety-provoking VR experiences. Their studies show "a lasting psychological impact after subjects return to the physical world."[43] Children are especially susceptible to negative VR experiences, so their exposure to VR should be limited. "Parents need to be careful,

CRIME IN VIRTUAL WORLDS

One of the potential trouble areas that has come to light with virtual reality is the possibility that people can commit crimes while in virtual environments. If multiple people are in a virtual environment, the chance exists that people can physically or mentally traumatize each other in that world. An assault or other crime committed in a virtual environment can carry over into the real world, causing psychological trauma for the crime victim. In one example from 2007, a seventeen-year-old Dutch boy was arrested on suspicion of stealing virtual furniture from other players in a virtual hotel called the Habbo Hotel. In the Habbo world, users create characters and play games. Players can buy furniture for their virtual rooms by spending real money. Even though the stolen furniture was virtual, the teenager was arrested because the furniture that he allegedly stole had been purchased with real money. Although the theft happened virtually, it was considered an actual theft by law. The boy was also suspected of violating a law by stealing players' passwords to access their accounts. US laws currently focus on the physical world rather than the virtual world. However, that may change as people spend more and more of their time online in virtual worlds.

active and participating, because the VR medium is more powerful than traditional media," Bailenson says.[44]

There are several other ways VR may be unhealthy. Instead of bringing people together, VR may encourage addictive behavior and isolation, disconnecting users from friends and family. People addicted to virtual reality may spend many hours in VR and prefer to spend time in VR rather than with people in the real world. Like the Internet, VR worlds include social networking, gambling, and gaming—all of which can be addictive. Dr. David Greenfield of the University of Connecticut School of Medicine treats people who are addicted to digital media. He confirms that the number of people addicted to technology is growing. "The numbers of referral and patients that we get calls from has gone up 10-fold in the last 20 years. We have had a 1,000 percent increase in the number of cases, and we treat hundreds of cases a year at this point," Greenfield says.[45] Authors Jim Blascovich and Jeremy Bailenson agree that for some people, VR could easily become addictive. "If Internet addictions are strong, addictions stemming from immersive virtual reality experiences should be even stronger," they wrote.[46] Finding satisfaction in virtual worlds instead of in real life leads to isolation and a loss of personal relationships. "The Internet and virtual realities easily satisfy such social needs and drives—sometimes so satisfying that addicted users will withdraw physically from society," Blascovich and Bailenson wrote.[47] By its very nature, VR is supposed to provide an opportunity to escape into other worlds. But it's still unknown whether long-term use of VR will change social behaviors. John Hanke, CEO of game-maker Niantic, agreed that the appealing aspects of VR can have negative effects. "I'm afraid [virtual reality] can be too good, in the sense of being an experience that people want to spend a huge amount of time in," he said.[48]

Experts believe that spending too much time with virtual reality could cause social isolation. Like other modern technologies, virtual reality has the potential for addictive use.

PRIVACY CONCERNS

Many types of technology track various data about users and their habits. Companies that make software and hardware can sometimes collect this information. When people register their new VR hardware and software products, VR companies collect personal information about who the users are. Companies also use small files called cookies to gather data about the programs users are looking at and how they are using the applications. Software beacons that allow a device to communicate with a server also transmit and store data. Companies use the data to understand how people use their software and hardware. User information helps companies customize their marketing and advertising to better target user preferences.

Many VR companies are international, so user data is spread to other countries where laws governing privacy may not be the same as in the US. This means companies in other countries may be able to use personal data in ways not allowed by US law. Many users are uncomfortable sharing their information, particularly name and location, with corporations. In addition to this basic data, VR companies can collect information gathered from VR controllers and sensors. This data describes how users move their bodies in VR as well as the size of the room where the VR experience is taking place. Personal information that is not properly protected exposes users to privacy issues and security **breaches**. VR user accounts, including payment information, may be hacked. Businesses that use VR are also at risk of someone stealing work made in virtual reality environments. "For example, if I'm in an enterprise and there's a headset, do I want someone to steal my headset? Do I want someone to take the headset,

and put it on, and see the collaborative thing I'm doing?" asked Frank Soqui of Intel Corporation.[49] As with any emerging technology, privacy and security concerns regarding virtual reality may take some time to develop as problems become more obvious with use. VR is still so new that it is difficult to know what types of security measures are adequate. "As these new technologies are being rushed to market, the appropriate privacy and security considerations are not being adhered to or paid attention to," said attorney Steven Teppler, an expert in electronic and technology law.[50] VR consumers—including organizations such as hospitals, schools, and businesses—need to be aware of potential security issues and take steps to protect their privacy.

Chapter 4

What Is the Future of Virtual Reality?

Despite concerns surrounding the technology, experts predict a bright future for virtual reality. New technological advancements will make virtual reality accessible to more people. These innovations will also bring about new applications that will impact many aspects of daily life.

UPGRADED GEAR AND LOWER COST

If VR technology is to become mainstream and make a greater impact on society, it must overcome several hurdles. VR gear is still expensive for many consumers. Sophisticated VR devices require users to have powerful computers or game consoles. Headsets can cost $400 to $600, while computers and consoles can cost hundreds or even thousands of dollars more. There is also the issue of limited content. People don't want to spend money on expensive VR gear when there are just a few applications for them to use. In turn, VR developers do not want to spend money producing content if there are too few consumers willing to purchase it. Still, VR is making progress as companies, especially large corporations such as Facebook and HTC, continue to fund research and development and tackle the obstacles that stand in the way of VR going mainstream.

One problem with current virtual reality technology is that it needs to be more **ergonomic**. Consumers complain of heavy headsets that cause neck strain. Some headsets don't fit properly, are difficult to adjust, and make users feel hot and sweaty. Most high-end VR headsets must be attached to computers and game consoles by cords and cables. Being tethered to another device can diminish the immersive VR experience. "The problem with the cord is if a user is effectively locked into a box,

restricted by the cord, it essentially defeats the purpose of having them immersed in a supposed 360-degree environment. This industry won't work if you're tethered to a PC. It won't work unless you can experience things the way you do in real life," says John Riccitiello, CEO of Unity, a company that produces digital content.[51] For VR to progress, headsets need to become smaller, more comfortable, less expensive, and wireless.

Advances in wireless VR will free users from wrestling with cable connections. While mobile VR headsets such as Google Cardboard and Daydream View exist, these headsets do not have the sophistication and processing power of HMDs connected to consoles and personal computers. WiGig is a promising wireless transmission technology that uses higher frequency radio signals than Wi-Fi. By accessing these frequencies, WiGig transmits data from the computer to the headset at high speeds with minimal latency or delay. WiGig wireless technology quickly transmits content such as streaming audio and video over short distances. In January 2018, HTC announced a partnership with electronics giant Intel Corporation to produce a WiGig upgrade kit. The kit uses a chargeable wireless adapter that attaches to Vive and Vive Pro headsets. With the adapter, users do not have to connect their headsets to consoles. "Wireless VR has been on nearly every VR user's wish list since the technology was unveiled. By collaborating with HTC to commercialize Intel's WiGig technology, we will guarantee that wireless VR meets the most discerning quality bar for home users and business VR customers," says Intel Corporation's Frank Soqui.[52]

Wireless VR headsets create a more immersive and comfortable VR experience. Users have the freedom to make quick movements without being restricted by cables and cords. Wireless headgear still requires movement tracking devices to be placed around a room to follow user actions. But companies such as Chirp Microsystems are working on a technology called inside-out tracking which gives VR headsets the ability to track users' movements without external sensing devices. These wireless VR headsets would use ultrasound sensors instead. VR companies are also improving screen display resolution and graphics to eliminate "the screen-door effect." This phenomenon occurs when digital images are so large that viewers see lines between pixels on a screen. Viewers feel as though they are looking at images through a screen door. Refresh rate also affects image clarity. To see motion in a video, a series of images are projected onscreen at a rapid rate. Refresh rate refers to the number of images shown per second. If the images are displayed fast enough, the brain is fooled into seeing motion. High refresh rates mean images will be smooth and realistic. New HMD displays are being developed with increased pixel count and faster refresh rates that improve display images. These display improvements will also help reduce the problem of VR sickness, which keeps some people from using virtual reality.

Like HTC, Oculus is also producing improved wireless headsets. In 2018, Oculus released Oculus Go, its first standalone VR headset. The improved headset is lightweight and made from soft, breathable fabric. Oculus Go also touts a high-resolution screen that is clearer than previous screens, reduces glare, and has a wide field of view.

Oculus Rift was one of the first prominent virtual reality headsets for consumers. Oculus released a new, lighter headset called Oculus Go in 2018.

The headset contains built-in speakers that add to a more realistic immersive experience. However, the Oculus Go lacks the positional tracking capabilities of the Rift. The Oculus Go was created as an affordable choice for consumers. Oculus is also developing the wireless Santa Cruz HMD. Not only is the Santa Cruz mobile, but it also offers two positional-tracking hand controllers with "six degrees of freedom" (6DOF). This technology can follow a greater range of hand movements, promising to create a seamless experience for users. Better haptics will also make virtual reality more immersive and deliver the presence that sets VR apart from other media. As companies pursue improvements in VR hardware, they are also looking for ways to make VR more affordable for consumers and businesses. VR is expected to grow in the coming years, which will help drive down costs and make VR more accessible. And the more widespread VR is, the more impact it will have on people's lives.

Several major virtual reality companies are partnering with academic institutions. They hope to tap into the knowledge and creativity of students and faculty to advance all aspects of virtual reality. In January 2018, the University of Washington received $6 million to launch the UW Reality Lab in Seattle. Three companies—Facebook, Google, and Huawei—are funding the lab, which will be one of the world's first virtual and **augmented reality** (AR) academic centers. The lab will focus on creating new VR technologies as well as educating the next generation of VR professionals. UW professor and lab cofounder Steve Seitz says:

> We're seeing some really compelling and high-quality AR and VR experiences being built today. But there are still many core research advances needed to move the industry forward—tools for easily creating content, infrastructure solutions for streaming 3D video, and privacy and security safeguards—that university researchers are uniquely positioned to tackle.[53]

THE FUTURE OF ENTERTAINMENT

At the Eastridge Mall in San Jose, California, four teens wearing mobile VR headsets and using hand controllers played a VR game outside a Sears department store. In the VR world of *Prism Break*, the teens became colored cartoon cats with square faces. As white blocks whizzed by them, the teens worked together as a team to smash the blocks and score points. The game was part of the Eastridge Mall's temporary pop-up arcade, which was made by roping off an area inside the mall. Temporary and permanent virtual reality arcades are opening around the world. "People are seeing the business opportunity [in virtual reality arcades]. There are cafes in South Korea that are destinations, where teams of people will go and eat and play and socialize—arcades by definition are a social experience," says Intel's Soqui.[54] One of the most popular entertainment VR experiences is called Zero Latency. The free-roam VR experience takes place in 2,000–4,000-square-foot (190–370 sq m) centers that accommodate groups of up to eight people. Wearing mobile headsets and carrying simulated weapons and game controllers, players team up to complete missions in a virtual world of their choosing. Eighteen centers are located around the world including in the United States, Australia, Malaysia, and Spain.

VR World is a 15,000-square-foot (1,400 sq m) multi-level permanent arcade that opened in New York City in 2017. Advertised as "the largest virtual reality experience center located in North America and the Western Hemisphere," the arcade offers a multitude of games as well as a floor with film, music, and art, a bar, and food service.[55] Big-screen TVs allow everyone to watch and be a part of the VR experience, even without a headset. Trained VR guides help guests get acquainted with VR at each station.

Arcades are just one example of how VR is changing trends in location-based entertainment (LBE). LBEs are entertainment experiences that take place in community spaces outside the home. Examples of LBEs are arcades, amusement parks, and movie theaters. In the early days of the Internet, many people could not afford to buy expensive computer equipment and software. Instead, they gathered at Internet cafes, where they could use computers. Similarly, virtual reality–based LBE is making VR accessible to a wider audience. At arcades, people who have never used virtual reality or who cannot afford VR equipment have an opportunity to try out the technology. Virtual arcades don't just cater to teens who want to play games. Many also rent space for businesses to use for VR experiences. Gaming is still a primary driving force behind advancements in virtual reality hardware and content. Arcades expose more people to the world of VR, helping to promote the technology. "You can walk in and try some of the best of what virtual reality has to offer. What we're trying to do is make virtual reality accessible to consumers," says Yasser Ghanchi, CEO of VR World.[56] Arcades are also dispelling the notion that virtual reality creates social isolation. Several of the stations at VR World are flight and racing car simulators that can only be used in an arcade environment. "We want this to be accessible to consumers and lead to wider VR adoption, but we also want to partner with [VR content developers] because they need support," Ghanchi says.[57] By bringing virtual reality to the public on a large scale, arcades and other location-based VR experiences help fuel consumer interest as well as content development. They are also generating a social environment where people can connect with each other through virtual reality.

The movie-making industry is just starting to venture into the world of LBE virtual reality. Major Hollywood entertainment studios and media companies, including Comcast, Sony, Fox, Lucasfilm, and Disney, are embracing VR and investing millions of dollars in the industry. "We're always searching for the next great computing platform, and VR is a very good suspect," says Michael Yang, managing director of Comcast Ventures.[58] Creating movies in VR requires a combined effort between industries. Movie producers work with VR content and hardware companies to create VR movie experiences.

In conjunction with the 2016 release of the remake of the *Ghostbusters* movie, Utah-based VR corporation The Void teamed

Virtual reality is being incorporated into many different group entertainment activities, such as the Ghostbusters: Dimension *exhibit in New York City. These activities encourage people to socialize together while using VR.*

up with Sony Pictures to create *Ghostbusters: Dimension* in New York City. The VR experience lets teams of up to four players become Ghostbusters who wander around hunting ghosts in a New York apartment building. The experience is billed as "hyper-reality." "This is not about watching 'Ghostbusters.' It's about being a Ghostbuster," says Hollywood director Ivan Reitman.[59] Players wearing haptic vests can move and interact with objects in real world sets and receive responses in the virtual landscape. So far, VR movies last fifteen minutes or less. VR movies are still in the experimental stage. As the technology and content becomes more sophisticated, VR movies may be the future of cinema. But some say VR content still needs to become more compelling in order for virtual reality to make a greater impact. "A headset is a paperweight without good content," says Loren Hammonds, who oversees the selection of virtual reality projects for the Tribeca Film Festival in New York City.[60] Companies are forging ahead to create a wider variety of content for their devices.

NEW JOBS IN VIRTUAL REALITY

As the business of virtual reality grows, new types of jobs are being created in many business sectors. Companies that create virtual reality experiences are emerging, and they need people to develop VR hardware and software. In response, some high schools are adding classes to familiarize students with virtual reality. Schools want students to prepare for work in a technical world where computer skills and knowledge of technologies such as virtual reality are vital. Michael Carbenia is the director of career and technical education for the Saint Lucie, Florida, public schools. He has implemented virtual reality and other computer technologies into school programs to give students real-life skills they will need to compete for jobs in today's technology-driven job market. Carbenia says:

> [The students are] getting the accurate training they need, and I think that puts them at a huge advantage over a student who is still doing it the traditional way. We also want to prepare our students for jobs that don't exist yet. We want them to have some fundamental skills they're comfortable with, and I believe working in a virtual reality environment is one of those skills.[61]

Many colleges are adding classes and degree programs in virtual reality. Florida's Ringling College of Art and Design began offering a degree in virtual reality development in fall 2018, becoming the first art college to offer such a program. Jim McCampbell who heads Ringling's computer animation department, says:

Thanks to recent, incredible strides in technology, virtual reality has become a new medium. We are excited to be forging into this new area that has so much potential for reshaping how we think about storytelling experiences. The ability to tell stories from multiple points of view and the ability to move the viewer from a role of spectator to that of a participant will serve as a brand-new canvas for artists and designers. Ringling College's world-renowned reputation for the fusion of art and technology make this the perfect place to launch such a cutting-edge major.[62]

NEW POSSIBILITIES THROUGH EYE-TRACKING TECHNOLOGY

Swedish company Tobii is developing sophisticated eye-tracking technology for use in virtual reality headsets. HMDs with eye tracking allow users to make things happen in virtual worlds just by looking at them. Eye tracking works on the premise that what a user intends to do is closely tied to what they are looking at. Eye tracking enables users to focus on objects in the virtual world to get a response. Viewers can make eye contact with their avatars and with other characters. When a user blinks, so does his or her avatar. When they make eye contact with characters in VR, the characters also make eye contact and respond. Accurate eye contact has the potential to enhance social interactions in VR. Eye focus can also be used to select buttons in VR just by looking at them. Eye tracking also makes it possible for HMDs to focus processing power on the area where the user is looking. This allows the HMD to concentrate high-quality graphics in that spot instead of on the whole scene, producing a better display, especially on slower VR systems. HMDs with eye tracking can also adjust VR images to align with the user's pupils. This produces better-quality images and makes the VR experience more comfortable for the viewer. Viewers can also use eye tracking to navigate and make selections by looking at what they want and clicking with a controller. HMDs with eye trackers have the potential to vastly improve VR immersion and performance.

As the number of ways to use virtual reality increases, so do employment opportunities associated with the industry. "The virtual reality space is taking off, and I believe the job opportunities are only going to grow in the next few years," says Nate Beatty, cofounder of IrisVR, a company that creates VR for architecture, engineering, and construction.[63] As the VR industry blossoms, there is a need for programmers, engineers, product managers, project managers, and others who specialize in VR technology. Many of the skills that computer professionals have are transferable to VR technology. For instance, software developers have been around for decades, but now they can choose to work specifically with virtual reality applications. Hardware engineers work with the physical components of VR technology. They may design HMDs, haptic devices, and other parts that transmit VR images. Virtual reality programs require 360-degree video. New companies are emerging that only produce 360-video and other images for VR.

CHANGING HUMAN BEHAVIOR

While violent and frightening VR experiences can cause real-life aggression and anxiety, VR can also positively change human behavior through immersive storytelling. The annual Tribeca Film Festival in New York highlights projects that merge filmmaking, technology, and storytelling. The festival's Virtual Arcade and Storyscapes incorporates several virtual reality films. The immersive nature of virtual reality films is proving to be a powerful medium that can influence people's emotions, thoughts, and actions as it draws viewers into the storyline. Many documentary filmmakers are using VR to evoke **empathy** from their audiences. In 2017, the VR film *The Last Goodbye* premiered at the Tribeca Film Festival. It featured Holocaust survivor Pinchas Gutter as he toured the Majdanek Concentration Camp in Poland in July 2016. Viewers walked alongside Gutter as he he shared the horrors he and his family suffered. Filmmakers used tens of thousands of photographs of the site as well as video of Gutter walking at the location to create the emotionally powerful, immersive experience. By immersing the audience in

the story and bringing them into another person's experience, virtual reality can connect people and help them understand each other's plight. "We are entering an era that is unprecedented in human history, where you can transform the self and [you can] experience anything the animator can fathom. The research shows it can have a deep effect on behavior," says VR expert Jeremy Bailenson.[64]

Another virtual reality film, *Clouds Over Sidra*, transports the audience to a refugee camp in northern Jordan. Viewers experience a day in the life of a young Syrian girl named Sidra as she narrates. Even though the film lasts just eight-and-a-half minutes, it has been a powerful tool for advocacy. Chris Milk, who created the film, showed it to decision-makers at the United Nations (UN) in an effort to help them understand the dire situation of Syrians in refugee camps. The UN followed up by equipping fundraisers for the United Nations Children's Fund (UNICEF) with Google Cardboard viewers that showed a brief two-minute clip of the film. After potential donors saw the clip, donations to UNICEF doubled. A 2017 Nielsen report on how virtual reality ads affected people's charitable donations proves that VR can positively affect people's charitable giving behavior. The analysis showed that 48 percent of people who viewed VR content about a nonprofit were likely to donate to the cause. Of the people who viewed non-VR content, only 38 percent would consider donating to the charity. In tests that measured recall of charity advertisements, 84 percent of the people who viewed virtual reality ads were able to recall the brand. Even though the percentage of people likely to donate was not 100 percent, the results showed that virtual reality does have a positive impact on how consumers view a charity's cause. These results are pushing some nonprofits to consider using more VR content in the future. Comparing the results of virtual reality charity ads versus traditional ads, Harry Brisson, director of lab research at Nielsen says:

> It's important to remember that VR is still in an embryonic stage as a medium, so to already see such strong performance from VR relative to more traditional ad formats is an encouraging sign for the pioneers making content today. With continued research and improvement, these experiences will only continue to improve, benefiting consumers, creators, and the charities they support.[65]

Milk has made several other virtual reality documentaries. In a 2015 TED Talk about virtual reality, Milk emphasized the power of the medium to influence human behavior. "It connects humans to other humans in a profound way that I've never seen before in any other form of media. And it can change people's perception of each other. And that's how I think virtual reality has the potential to actually change the world," Milk says.[66]

VR corporations Oculus and HTC Vive also promote the use of virtual reality to support humanitarian and environmental causes. In 2016, Oculus began VR for Good, a program aimed at using virtual reality to inspire social change. The program paired ten rising filmmakers with ten nonprofits. The teams worked together to create virtual reality films that showcased their organizations' missions. Similarly, HTC Vive's VR for Impact is a multi-year program that funds

Virtual reality films have been featured in film festivals all over the world. VR films have also been used for advocacy

virtual reality projects that benefit the greater good. These projects focus on making the UN's seventeen sustainable development goals a reality. The goals target ways to improve living conditions worldwide by ending poverty, hunger, inequality, and injustice, as well as protecting the planet and promoting peace. Funded projects include OrthoVR, LIFE, and *Tree*. OrthoVR makes it possible for medical professionals in developing countries to quickly and easily create prosthetic limbs using virtual reality technology. Using virtual reality, clinicians can design limbs in 3D, shaping and perfecting them before they are printed with a 3D printer. The LIFE project connects health care workers with trainers in a virtual hospital. In the hospital's realistic setting, workers can learn to deal with medical emergencies.

Tree premiered at the Sundance Film Festival in 2017. In this immersive film, viewers become a kapok tree growing in the Amazon.

Viewers' bodies become the tree trunk and their arms become branches. To achieve a full-body haptic experience, users wear special sleeves on their arms and a pack that produces vibrations. They also stand on a vibrating floor. An air blower and heaters create the feeling of wind and fire. VR designers Yedan Qian and Xin Liu were part of the team that created *Tree*. They describe the reaction of audiences who have experience the film: "We've seen audiences coming out of the VR film experience in tears. It's been exhilarating for us to witness the power of body sensations in this new form of storytelling. People have told us they really felt like the tree and found its destruction to be terrifying and emotional."[67]

CONNECTING IN VIRTUAL REALITY

Another growing area of virtual reality involves platforms that allow people to meet and spend time together. Social platforms bring users together from all over the world. In 2017, Facebook introduced Spaces, a social virtual reality app that can be used with Oculus headsets. With Spaces, Facebook wants to dispel the notion that VR is only for people interested in gaming and technology. The social app is meant to broaden the reach of VR and introduce people to using VR specifically as a means for connecting with one another. "We really want people outside of VR to feel like it's for them," says Rachel Franklin, Facebook's head of social VR.[68] To use Spaces, people must have an Oculus headset, Oculus Touch controllers, and a Facebook account. Four friends at a time can meet in Spaces around a virtual table. The experience lets people talk to each other, take selfies, draw with a virtual marker, and view 360-degree photos and videos. It allows users to see body language, an important cue in communication that makes the interaction feel more realistic. Users in VR can receive phone calls from people who aren't using VR via the Messenger app. One of the main objectives of Spaces is to allow people to communicate with each other in virtual reality and make VR a social experience where people get together and interact. "This is really a new communication platform. By feeling truly present, you can share unbounded spaces and experiences with the people in your life," says Mark Zuckerberg, Facebook CEO.[69] Facebook Spaces is available to the public as a **beta app**. It still has many limitations to overcome before it is more widely adopted by users. Currently, Spaces is limiting because not many people own Oculus VR equipment. There are also a limited number of options of what people can do once they meet in Spaces. Developers hope to expand the platform, perhaps allowing users to connect with people who aren't their Facebook friends. "Everything we do should really be facilitating your interaction with someone else, or enhancing that relationship somehow," Franklin says.[70]

As virtual reality becomes more sophisticated, people are discovering more ways to apply the technology to everyday life. VR has already made inroads in several fields, including education, medicine, business, and entertainment. If virtual reality is to become a part of everyone's daily life, equipment needs to be more user friendly and affordable. But even as progress is made, the future of VR is uncertain. VR expert Bailenson believes that "as the technology improves and the creation tools develop, the range of ways people can express themselves in VR, and the applications they can build with it, will be bounded only by their imagination."[71] Innovations in virtual reality technology and software are moving forward at a rapid pace, ensuring that virtual reality will have a lasting impact on future society.

Source Notes

Introduction: Virtual Reality Today

1. Quoted in Noelle McGee, "AT&T Launches Annual Anti-Distracted-Driving Campaign at Danville High," *The News-Gazette*, February 14, 2018. www.news-gazette.com.

2. Quoted in "New Virtual Reality App Highlights Distraction Risk by Taking Young Drivers on Crash Course That Ends with Date in Court," *Ford Media Center*, October 6, 2017. media.ford.com.

3. Quoted in Colm Hebblethwaite, "How Aceable Aims to Integrate VR into Driver Education," *VR360*, June 2, 2017. www.virtualreality-news.net.

4. Quoted in Dave McNary, "Paramount Partners with Bigscreen for 'Top Gun' Virtual Reality Showings," *Variety*, December 20, 2017. www.variety.com.

5. Jeremy Bailenson, *Experience on Demand: What Virtual Reality Is, How It Works, and What It Can Do*. New York: W.W. Norton & Company, 2018. p. 12.

Chapter 1: What Is the Technology behind Virtual Reality?

6. Daniel Newman, "CES 2017: How Immersive Virtual Reality Points to the Future of Product and Experience Design," *Forbes*, January 8, 2017. www.forbes.com.

7. Quoted in Peter Ray Allison, "Virtual Reality Comes of Age in Manufacturing," *Computer Weekly,* February 2015. www.computerweekly.com.

8. Quoted in "Sensorama Simulator Patent," *Google Patents*, patents.google.com.

9. Quoted in Bruce Sterling, "Augmented Reality: 'The Ultimate Display' by Ivan Sutherland, 1965," *Wired,* September 20, 2009. www.wired.com.

10. Quoted in Paul James, "Watch the 'Godfather of VR' Ivan Sutherland Speak at the 2015 Proto Awards," *Road to VR*, September 23, 2015. www.roadtovr.com.

11. Quoted in Elyse Betters, "Virtual Reality: Lessons from the Past for Oculus Rift," *BBC*, August 30, 2013. www.bbc.com.

12. Mark Zuckerberg, *Facebook*, March 25, 2014. www.facebook.com.

Chapter 2: How Does Virtual Reality Positively Impact Society?

13. Quoted in Maria Taylor, "Google Takes Novi Woods Students on 3-D Experience," *Hometown Life*, February 19, 2018. www.hometownlife.com.

14. Quoted in Taylor, "Google Takes Novi Woods Students on 3-D Experience."

15. Quoted in Heather Hansman, "How Can Schools Use Virtual Reality?" *Smithsonian*, February 3, 2016. www.smithsonianmag.com.

16. Quoted in Michele Molnar, "Google for Education Launches Beta for 'Create Your Own' Virtual Reality Experience," *EdWeek Market Brief*, January 27, 2018. marketbrief.edweek.org.

17. Quoted in Olivia Martin, "First U.S. Exhibition Devoted to Pierre Chareau Opens at NYC Jewish Museum," *The Architects Newspaper,* November 2, 2016. www.archpaper.com.

18. Quoted in Courtney Rothbard, "Smithsonian American Art Museum Releases 'Renwick Gallery WONDER 360' Virtual Reality App," *Smithsonian American Art Museum*, October 4, 2016. americanart.si.edu.

19. Quoted in John Gaudiosi, "How Ford Goes Further with Virtual Reality," *Fortune*, September 23, 2015. www.fortune.com.

20. Quoted in "Virtual Reality for Architecture: A Beginner's Guide," *AEC Magazine*, February 16, 2017. www.aecmag.com.

21. Quoted in "Virtual Reality for Architecture: A Beginner's Guide."

22. Quoted in Sam Lubell, "VR Is Totally Changing How Architects Dream Up Buildings," *Wired*, November 9, 2016. www.wired.com.

23. Quoted in DrivingTheNation, "Volvo & Google Create a Virtual Test Drive in the XC90," *YouTube*, November 25, 2014. www.youtube.com.

24. Quoted in Lowe's Home Improvement, "Lowe's Innovation Labs: The Next-Generation Lowe's Holoroom," *YouTube*, October 29, 2016. www.youtube.com.

25. Quoted in Lowe's Home Improvement, "Lowe's Innovation Labs: The Next-Generation Lowe's Holoroom."

26. Quoted in Rob Marvin, "Why a Rockstar Games Founder Is All-In on Safety-Focused VR," *PC Magazine*, January 25, 2018. www.pcmag.com.

27. Quoted in Marvin, "Why a Rockstar Games Founder Is All-In on Safety-Focused VR."

28. Quoted in Marvin, "Why a Rockstar Games Founder Is All-In on Safety-Focused VR."

29. Quoted in Cat Zakrzewski, "Virtual Reality Takes On the Videoconference," *The Wall Street Journal*, September 18, 2016. www.wsj.com.

30. Quoted in Charlie Hall, "How The 101st Airborne Trains in Virtual Reality," *Polygon*, October 7, 2014. www.polygon.com.

31. Quoted in "The Stanford Virtual Heart—Revolutionizing Education on Congenital Heart Defects," *Stanford Children's Health*, n.d., www.stanfordchildrens.org.

32. Quoted in UCSF Benioff Children's Hospital Oakland, "Virtual Reality (VR) Pain Relief at UCSF Benioff Children's Hospital Oakland," *YouTube*, August 23, 2016. www.youtube.com.

33. Quoted in UCSF Benioff Children's Hospital Oakland, "Virtual Reality (VR) Pain Relief at UCSF Benioff Children's Hospital Oakland."

34. Quoted in UCSF Benioff Children's Hospital Oakland, "Virtual Reality (VR) Pain Relief at UCSF Benioff Children's Hospital Oakland."

Chapter 3: How Does Virtual Reality Negatively Impact Society?

35. Quoted in Tyler Wilde, "Man Dies in VR Accident, Reports Russian News Agency," *PC Gamer*, December 22, 2017. www.pcgamer.com.

36. Quoted in Becca Caddy, "Vomit Reality: Why VR Makes Some of Us Feel Sick and How to Make It Stop," *Wareable*, October 19, 2016. www.wareable.com.

37. Quoted in Sandee LaMotte, "The Very Real Health Dangers of Virtual Reality," *CNN*, December 13, 2017. www.cnn.com.

38. Bailenson, *Experience on Demand: What Virtual Reality Is, How It Works, and What It Can Do*, p. 59.

39. Quoted in Jeff Grabmeier, "Immersed in Violence: How 3-D Gaming Affects Video Game Players," *Ohio State University*, October 19, 2014. news.osu.edu.

40. Quoted in Simon Parkin, "The Coming Horror of Virtual Reality," *The New Yorker*, May 15, 2016. www.newyorker.com.

41. Quoted in Parkin, "The Coming Horror of Virtual Reality."

42. Quoted in LaMotte, "The Very Real Health Dangers of Virtual Reality."

43. Quoted in Parkin, "The Coming Horror of Virtual Reality."

44. Quoted in LaMotte, "The Very Real Health Dangers of Virtual Reality."

45. Quoted in Barbara Booth, "Internet Addiction Is Sweeping America, Affecting Millions," *CNBC*, August 29, 2017. www.cnbc.com.

46. Jim Blascovich and Jeremy Bailenson, *Infinite Reality*, New York: William Morrow, 2011. p. 183.

47. Blascovich and Bailenson, *Infinite Reality*, p. 190.

48. Quoted in Tim Bajarin, "I Love Virtual Reality, but I'm Also Afraid of It," *Time*, May 16, 2017. www.time.com.

49. Quoted in Chris Wiltz, "5 Major Challenges for VR to Overcome," *Design News*, April 28, 2017. www.designnews.com.

50. Quoted in Marianne Kolbasuk McGee, "Virtual Reality: Real Privacy and Security Risks," *Data Breach Today*, June 16, 2016. www.databreachtoday.com.

Chapter 4: What Is the Future of Virtual Reality?

51. Quoted in Wiltz, "5 Major Challenges for VR to Overcome."

52. Quoted in Kevin Carbotte, "HTC Vive WiGig Wireless Upgrade Is Coming in Q3 2018," *Tom's Guide*, January 9, 2018. www.tomsguide.com.

53. Quoted in Jennifer Langston, "UW Reality Lab Launches with $6M from Tech Companies to Advance Augmented and Virtual Reality Research," *UW News*, January 8, 2018. www.washington.edu.

54. Quoted in Zara Stone, "The Business of Virtual Reality Arcades, a Future $45 Billion Industry," *Forbes*, August 2, 2017. www.forbes.com.

55. Quoted in Christopher Robbins, "They Have Seen the Future and It's Wasting Zombies at the Arcade," *The New York Times*, January 17, 2018. www.nytimes.com.

56. Quoted in Eva Kis, "Giant Virtual Reality Arcade VR World Opens in Midtown," *Metro US*, July 15, 2017. www.metro.us.

57. Quoted in Kis, "Giant Virtual Reality Arcade VR World Opens in Midtown."

58. Quoted in Steven Zeitchik, "Big Hollywood Begins to Place Its Chips on Virtual Reality—but Is It a Smart Bet?" *Los Angeles Times*, July 15, 2016. www.latimes.com.

59. Quoted in Zeitchik, "Big Hollywood Begins to Place Its Chips on Virtual Reality—but Is It a Smart Bet?"

60. Quoted in Marty Swant, "What Needs to Come First for VR to Take Off, Mass Hardware Adoption or Compelling Content?" *AdWeek*, January 7, 2018. www.adweek.com.

61. Quoted in Wendy McMahon, "How AR and VR Prepare Students for Jobs of the Future (and Save Districts Money)," *EdSurge*, January 29, 2018. www.edsurge.com.

62. Quoted in Ringling College of Art and Design, "Ringling College Becomes First Art + Design School to Offer Virtual Reality Development BFA," *Global Newswire*, October 18, 2017. www.globalnewswire.com.

63. Quoted in Caroline Zaayer Kaufman, "How to Land a Job in Virtual Reality Tech," *Monster*, n.d. www.monster.com.

64. Quoted in Jennifer Alsever, "Is Virtual Reality the Ultimate Empathy Machine?" *Wired*, n.d. www.wired.com.

65. Quoted in "Virtual Empathy: How 360-Degree Video Can Boost the Efforts of Non-Profits," *Nielsen Insights*, May 10, 2017. www.nielsen.com.

66. Chris Milk, "How Virtual Reality Can Create the Ultimate Empathy Machine," *TED*, March 2015. www.ted.com.

67. Xin Liu and Yedan Qian, "If You Were a Tree," *MIT Media Lab*, June 13, 2017. www.media.mit.edu.

68. Quoted in Lisa Eadicicco, "Inside Facebook's Plan to Take Virtual Reality Mainstream," *Time*, August 2, 2017. www.time.com.

69. Quoted in Eadicicco, "Inside Facebook's Plan to Take Virtual Reality Mainstream."

70. Quoted in Eadicicco, "Inside Facebook's Plan to Take Virtual Reality Mainstream."

71. Bailenson, *Experience on Demand: What Virtual Reality Is, How It Works, and What It Can Do*, p. 259.

For Further Research

Books

John Allen, *Improving Virtual Reality*. San Diego, CA: ReferencePoint Press, 2018.

Jeremy Bailenson, *Experience on Demand: What Virtual Reality Is, How It Works, and What It Can Do*. New York: W.W. Norton & Company, 2018.

Carla Mooney, *What Is the Future of Virtual Reality?* San Diego, CA: ReferencePoint Press, 2017.

Tony Parisi, *Learning Virtual Reality: Developing Immersive Experiences and Applications for Desktop, Web, and Mobile*. Sebastopol, CA: O'Reilly Media, 2016.

Don Rauf, *Virtual Reality*. New York: Rosen Publishing, 2016.

James Roland, *Virtual Reality and Medicine*. San Diego, CA: ReferencePoint Press, 2018.

Internet Sources

Brendan Cassidy and David Robinson, "Virtual Reality Is Allowing Us to See Some of the World's Most Inaccessible Archeological Sites," *Smithsonian Magazine,* December 14, 2017. www.smithsonianmag.com.

Stuart Dredge, "The Complete Guide to Virtual Reality—Everything You Need to Get Started," *Guardian*, November 10, 2016. www.theguardian.com.

Rebecca Hersher, "NASA Taps Young People to Help Develop Virtual Reality Technology," *National Public Radio*, November 24, 2017. www.npr.org.

Lorne Manly, "A Virtual Reality Revolution, Coming to a Headset Near You," *The New York Times*, November 19, 2015. www.nytimes.com.

Jonathan Strickland, "How Virtual Reality Works," *HowStuffWorks*, n.d. www.howstuffworks.com.

Muhammad Usman, "7 Ways VR Is Improving Healthcare," *UploadVR*, March 7, 2018. www.uploadvr.com.

Websites

TechCrunch
https://beta.techcrunch.com

TechCrunch focuses on breaking news about the technology industry, including virtual reality. The site includes articles as well as videos.

Virtual Reality Society
www.vrs.org.uk

This website has news and information about virtual reality technologies. It includes sections that explain the history of virtual reality, its applications, and how it works.

VR360
www.virtualreality-news.net

This website offers the latest news about virtual and augmented reality trends.

Index

Index
Continued

Image Credits

About the Author

Cecilia Pinto McCarthy has written several science and technology books for young readers. She also teaches environmental science classes at a nature sanctuary. She lives with her family north of Boston, Massachusetts.